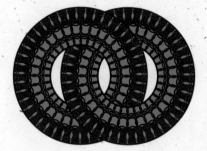

NEIGHBORHOOD REGISTER

NEIGHBORHOOD REGISTER

MARCUS JACKSON

POEMS

CavanKerry ◈ Press LTD.

CavanKerry Press Ltd.
Fort Lee, New Jersey
www.cavankerrypress.org

Library of Congress Cataloging-in-Publication Data

Jackson, Marcus, 1981-
Neighborhood register : poems / Marcus Jackson. -- 1st ed.
p. cm.
ISBN-13: 978-1-933880-25-9 (alk. paper)
ISBN-10: 1-933880-25-2 (alk. paper)
I. Title.

PS3610.A35427N45 2011
813'.6--dc22

2010046922

Cover art Jonathan Howard © 2011
Cover and interior design by Gregory Smith

First Edition 2011, Printed in the United States of America

NEW VOICES
CavanKerry❖Press

CavanKerry Press is dedicated to springboarding the careers
of previously unpublished poets by bringing to print two to
three New Voices annually. Manuscripts are selected from open
submission; CavanKerry Press does not conduct competitions.

CavanKerry Press is grateful for the support it receives
from the New Jersey State Council on the Arts.

 CONTENTS

3

Personal Thanks

To my wife, Nicole. Your presence heals however
the world may hurt.

To my vivid, crazy, passionate family.

To Timothy Geiger. I'm afraid to imagine how much
grimmer my life would be without knowing you.

To my ingenious, generous teachers and mentors:
Elizabeth Alexander, Rane Arroyo, Jane Bradley,
Cyrus Cassells, Kwame Dawes, Toi Derricotte,
Cornelius Eady, Thomas Sayers Ellis, Kimiko Hahn,
Edward Hirsch, Erica Hunt, Angela Jackson, Major Jackson,
Yusef Komunyakaa, Philip Levine, Phillis Levin, Glyn Maxwell,
Colleen J. McElroy, Sharon Olds, Ed Roberson,
Patricia Smith, and Susan Wheeler.

To Cave Canem, the warm house in the
middle of the wilderness.

FOREWORD

Although it doesn't name the city, Marcus Jackson's elegant
and eloquent first book registers the lives of people in a neigh-
borhood that exists in most American towns. Its people are
somewhere between middle and lower class. Their struggle
is tense, almost life or death, to master forces through which
they might easily lose their toehold. A register usually gives
us facts; it speaks to its readers, outsiders, from the outsid-
er's point of view; it speaks in the outsider's language. Here
is the register of one speaking from the inside; it is a profes-
sion of loyalty—the poet registering publicly who HE is and
what HE belongs to. He does so in language so intimate and
alive, that reading the poems is like smelling a pot of long
cooking greens on the back burner.

The poet makes his first appearance in the first poem,
"645 Phillips Ave," which sets the stage for the rest of the
book in tone and formal accomplishment, and proves Jack-
son's right to speak as an insider. It gauges the lives of those
who have lived and live inside a rented dwelling, a "house
whose staircase creaked / like the knees of the retired farm-
er / I imagined built it." Jackson uses metaphor, not only
to make us see the world in a new way, but to move our vi-
sion in a very specific direction. These poems give life to ev-
erything they describe, humanize every person and object,
seeing them with compassion, and, in fact, cherishing them
more so because of what they have endured:

"A row of our cars—crippled
or bleeding flammably."

"The quaky table"

Jackson also means this book to be a musical regis-
ter—that is, the range of a human voice on a musical instru-
ment, which, in this case, is poetry. His epigraph by Philip
Levine leads the way: "There is one / Deep full note for each
of us. / This is the first night of my life / I know we are mu-
sic." One of the most impressive aspects of the book is its
formal use of sound—rhyme and assonance, for example.
I have never seen onomatopoeia used so frequently and in
such thrilling ways:

"Through an old man's throat
breath scrapes, bray
of trashcans dragged out of alleyway."

There are frequent metaphors that tie together music
and the body, but also with common objects from this world,
instruments people labor with:

"a staunch organ of pistons."

The poet's determined gift is to transform the every-
day struggles of this neighborhood into music, as if making
music is the only way to confer meaning and insure that
this place will not be forgotten. There is a tension at the
center of the book, an unsolvable question: How do you stay
and leave at the same time? Jackson studies the people who
leave, intensely; mostly, he does not like what he sees.

"My granddad glides alone
in his copper Chrysler—rear
fenders winged like a murderous bird…

Every Saturday he escapes
to Adrian, Michigan, his
White mistress, their high
yellow daughter with flat black hair . . ."

A young boy works all his life and gets "Pegged fourth in the pro draft . . ."

"Seldom, now, does his Range
Rover appear—truck body
low, a phonograph nose
needled to a road."

Jackson writes about boys (like himself) in "Ode to the Scholarship:" "We clawed like trapped hawks / to win you." Yet the poem expresses more sorrow and rage in looking back then triumph and pride in accomplishment.

"you diverted us from:
. . . police Caprices' locked
backseats, motel rooms

with dented lampshades, towns
where bone and muscle and flesh best
most of the hidden electricity
our minds fight to emit."

While he is one of those who claw their way and escape, at the same time, he is one of those who cannot. In the last line of the poem, he uses "our," putting himself with those who are still fighting. How do you stay and go at the same time? This book is the answer.

Most first books by poets are autobiographical; they tell the story of childhood and growing up. While Jackson's book looks like autobiography on the surface, when you look closely, the poet is hardly ever at center stage. There is a

kind of humility in the voice, a way of stepping back so that
the light shines on the other, as if his main purpose for even
being in the poem is to direct our attention to what is REAL-
LY important. In "Mary at the Tattoo Shop" the "I" makes
an appearance in the last two lines to rub salve on the neck
of the girl, but not to his glory; it is mostly to give us insight
into the complicated aspects of the wound.

> "My finger glistened in salve
> as I reached for her swollen name."

In "Admission" the poet describes the first time he had
sex. It is with a "shy girl I knew from Civics class …" After-
ward, going back to his waiting friends, he knows they will
want to hear about his "kingly" conquest. But the poet ad-
mits, "I sidestepped inky / puddles, a lie about feeling kingly
/ knocked to life in my mind, then a loud / wind kicked, thin-
ning my coat to a sheet." About cold, we used to say: "The
Hawk is talking!" He realizes a nature that both causes him
to act and, at the same time, drags him unintentionally into
things far beyond his control, actions in which he is not par-
ticularly heroic, or even good. "Rest of the way, I walked
with my head down," he offers us in the last line.

This is the first book of a poet whose voice and message
we trust, one whose remarkable love, wisdom and skills are
perfectly matched. We, his readers, register this neighbor-
hood, which has been drawn with the finest point of lan-
guage. This is a singular and significant voice. You will not
forget this neighborhood, or this poet.

—*Toi Derricotte*

There is one
deep full note for each of us.
This is the first night of my life
I know we are music.

—*Philip Levine*

NEIGHBORHOOD REGISTER

645 PHILLIPS AVE.

House whose basement flooded
    during every rowdy rain. House
whose staircase creaked
        like the knees of the retired farmer
I imagined built it. My family rented it
    a century after he could've lived,

    ambulance garage adjacent,
sirens that breeched our sleep.
        Most my parents' fights
happened mornings, coffee maker prattling,
    birds pecking yard for food.
With sister and friends, I dragged

dad's ashtray Kools, pulls
        banked in the jagged snub before butt.
A crony borrowed my bedroom
    to bumble with Danielle Combs, Magnavox
lilting dubbed R&B.
        Some nights, by myself, I climbed

        out a window to sit
on moss-blotched roof
    and meld my eyes to sky.
Whoever owns this house
        has torn it down. A removal crew
has yet to truck up. Brown

mounds of ripped away planks,
          mortar in stray, gray strands,
plaster iron-balled to flour, disconnected
      intestine of pipes.
Why don't we find and lift
       a couple intact bricks,

       let them chalk our palms maroon,
let them convey the weight it takes
     to cog a wall, to tolerate
110 Ohio winters, let alone
       the sounds and the heat
each tenant pressed against it?

ESCAPE, 1961

My dad's dad glides alone
in his copper Chrysler—rear
fenders winged like a murderous bird—
up a stretch of 23 North,
flanked each side by reedy marsh.

He grins, the gold bridge
between two of his teeth glints
in angled sun and highway wind.
In the console tray, a Lucky
smolders like a departed thought;

he can't know exactly
how dank his lungs remain
from a younger living
dredging coal mines.
Every Saturday he escapes

to Adrian, Michigan, his
White mistress, their high
yellow daughter with flat black hair,
who climbs the neighbor's cherry tree,
bare feet and dirty fingers

as pluck by pluck she eats
the cool, crimson globes,
until her daddy's tires
rustle the driveway gravel
as if jerking her from a dream.

VISITATION

Through an old man's throat
breath scrapes, bray
of trashcans dragged out of alleyway.

Street bulbs hum at insects' pitch.

In a Chevy belly, motor stutters
before it snares ignition's sweet note.

So late, intersection signals
direct merely air,
worry's wandering particles.

At a 24-hour donut hutch,
dozens of glazed rise
in a mechanical colander,
kettle-depth fizzing sugary grease.

Out a third floor flat, a couple's
voices claw, argument
outdone only by the salty
body-knock that always follows.

Do any dreams
landscaping the dozing skulls
of this block's young
include sound?

Which octaves will uncombine and climb through
the indefinite worlds
they wake from and wake into?

15 YEARS OLD IN A STOLEN LINCOLN

My friend's cousin conked out,
drown by St. Ides.
We pinched the keys

from the pocket of his Dickies.
Born at the car's fender seams,
rust bit blue paint.

A couple hubcaps absent,
but it ran fine, engine
a staunch organ of pistons.

Pulling to a payphone,
we dialed every girl we knew
until two joined the journey.

Our hearts hurried
when we slid by police cars.
From snubbed-out ashtray butts

we dug the pungent nub
of an unfinished joint.
Songs on the radio

static-rasped, we rode
long into night,
past the dim stagger

of our fathers and uncles
leaving bars at closing.
Taking turns driving,

fading tennis shoes
gathered the give
and push of the pedals.

We were too busy
to see the sky,
dark cloak pinned up by stars,

while we steered and studied
the glow that rose
from the girls' July thighs.

VISITING MY GREAT AUNTIE; CHESTER, GA

In a car for 15 hours, I forget
my stiffening knees
when ground begins spilling
red at the road edges.
First time more south than Tennessee,
I slow to her low-roofed house,
built before woods where slight
mist increases the denseness.
Our stolen elders died here,
their stomachs ashen fists.
Our meal is grilled pig ribs,
biscuits, baked squash, peaches
soft-fleshed as dusk sun.
Sitting with Auntie; on porch chairs
I stare at her arm—brown skin
so many summers thicker
than my shallow yellow.
High grass in the distance
jostles with a breeze; day
creeps away; crickets vibrate
and introduce night—
sky soon a vast face
watching with an ivory eye.

ODE TO THE HATER

Your name on our caller ID
leers like a traffic ticket on a windshield.

Your rumors are determined as termites,
your tongue jumpy like a jarred roach.

The births of healthy, gleaming babies
twist you ill. June is your

November, miracles your disasters;
Obama's election hospitalized you.

Your eyes drip pleasure-tears
when a wrecking ball strikes a school.

Kind minds have labored centuries
to guess reasons for your presence,

to invent figurative scissors
and clip the knotted cloth

blindfolding you from typical bliss.
In minutes, dawn will reacquire

the sky. We're tired. Besides,
even if a bundle of money appeared

unmarked in your living room,
you'd curse the sorry world

for creating paper crisp enough
to cut your counting thumb.

40 OUNCE

Summer has salted
our neighborhood to thirst;
tar that patches the wounds of roofs
heats to sluggish bubbles;
sun obligates
paint on car hoods to blotch.

Emphasized by the light
inside corner-store beer coolers,
your malt lusters.

You're cold gold down throat.

Lush like storm-brim wind.

Foam-skinned as any cleansing.

Within thick glass, you swish oceanic
as we share you palm to palm.

You have helped
this dice game clank alive,
paper-wager and victory-rake,
players with obsidian eyes.

Through an uncurtained pane,
a music video is visible;
women's shimmer slurs
like jewelry worn on a passerby.

Neighbors here and there snore,
hallway walls tacked
with flea-market art, closets
dehydrated by moth repellent.
They leave us to you.
They could plead tomorrow
in churches whose pipes
ramble behind brittle plaster.

We drink you to the pale bottom,
we drink until night sinks
into skin like silk,
until graveyard cops
circle our block like a clock arm,
until blood slides
like alloy through veins,
until words hammer
from the anvil of the brain,
until America's
continental wheel unbolts
and everybody can see
we gleam like greased bearings.

LITTLE SISTER
—to Jessica

Remember when we moved
to the house on Phillips,
right before Christmas,
sidewalk and drive gauzed in ice,
dad and uncle Terry
unloading past dark
the tall, rented truck?
Three weeks later we started
a new school; we knew
only each other, you
in third grade, me fifth.
First day, dad called me
into the steamy
bathroom where he shaved.
"Take care a' your sister, boy.
Make sure nobody
gives her a hard time."

With other kids we waited—
front walk, for doors
to unlock into huge halls.
Tasha Davis, that popular sixth grader,
stood with her followers
in a circle beside us.
She did most the talking, breath
flaring winter vapor.
Not long until she noticed us,
unjarred a joke
about your pink snow boots.

It felt like a few
grasshoppers got let loose
in my chest. Tasha told us,
Don't be mad!
You didn't even slide
your eyes toward mine
before forcing
your hand against her face.
She fell through friends,
to cement where she began
crying, shaky fingers
touching the bloody lobe
an earring had ripped from.
An adult hall guard found us,
his face half awake.
He tried to grab your elbow,
pull you to the principal.
You yanked back, strode
unheld into a school you'd
never entered, morning light
caught in your curls like barbwire.

FRESHMAN AUDITION

The bus driver yanks the lever; doors part,
September morning breaking
through all the identical windows.
Mama's ginger gait
takes her to the closest open seat.

White stockings, pleated skirt
she sewed from a fabric-store pattern.
It's her first week in Toledo, first
day at the parochial school her folks
patched together tuition for.

Other kids clamor; the hulky engine
whines, and mama tilts
her head so that hair hides
her acne thatches.
In two weeks, she'll walk

onto the dusty auditorium stage,
the mostly empty audience seats
straight-rowed like the sockets of picked crops.
She'll force her face to smile
at the few faculty in front, then she'll strike

every note of *Do Right Woman*
so that even the rafters' motes rouse,
and a senior theater kid will leave
to uncork a story of how
that new green eyed girl from South Bend can sing.

9TH GRADE HUNGER AND LOVE

Sadie's boyfriend, Rodney, pushed
weed from a duplex on Upton Street.
With my cousin, I climbed
the plywood-mended stairwell,
wedged in my fist the dollars
for a Friday dime-sack.
Sadie answered, oval face
and maple eyes seizing
the hall's limited light.
At my cousin's we doctored
a foil pipe for our herb;
when the coughing ended
my lungs were quiet,
dry like retired canoes.
We played two-person Spades,
missing ace replaced
by a stand-in from a different deck.
At dusk, we stepped from the stoop
to 7-Eleven for food.
We shared pork rinds
and a lukewarm soda,
our walk languid
like wagon wheels through sand.
Rodney's DeVille circled the corner,
its grill a gold grin, Sadie,
not quite hidden by window tint,
sitting in shotgun's leather throne.
My cousin, yellow dust
on his chin from the hog rinds,
said, *I bet they goin' downtown for*

dinner. I tipped
the can high for a final
drop, perhaps hope's
last stubborn speck
that Sadie would soon decline
men whose hands knew
money like forests know moss,
that she might order Rodney to stop,
that she might jump out and run
to me, kid whose stomach
was a bag of acid and snacks,
my jean pockets exactly
as flat as empty envelopes.

MONEY IN JUNCTURES
—to CF

1

You first heard it
on the public bus, riders
releasing fare into the toll chamber—
clink and clank
like a hopscotch game
whose players wear tap-shoes.

2

In the grammar school boys' room,
Donny thunderstruck
your crew, unfolding
a robbery's results—
three iguana-green hundreds
you crept your forefinger toward,
expecting the cash would
puncture like a touched hologram.

3

A sideways moon sliver
hanging hammock-like, you shattered
cars' pilot windows
with spark plugs' porcelain torsos.
A flathead pried stereos, wires

dangling like roots of a pulled plant.
Each unit made you
50 cash, journeys
to department stores,
their entrance smells
mixtures of the half vanished
colognes and perfumes
grinning women misted.

4

Hustle loot long
refrained from, it still sings some.
Last night, at the convenience store
for medicine to cool
your fevered son, you could hear
the surveillance camera wasn't
buzzing like a live one would,
you could hear thirst
for sleep in the clerk's words,
you could hear the weighty clang
when the till jammed back
into the register, could hear
the grassy whispers
of money uneasy as prey.

LOCAL CAR MECHANIC

Your eyes only see right
in garage light, your grip leaves
pens black as if rolled in coal,
your coveralls duplicate
your frame, beltless
equator of the waist,
your boots could've survived
a mile of lava, your hair
a township of silvering spirals,
forehead a hickory plank
protecting encyclopedias
written in neurons:
caliper and rotor, strut butter,
water pump, spindle,
tie rod, gear box,
rocker arm, distributer.
At six, you risked a whippin'
to dissect your transistor—
your mama might've barged in,
you on the floor, screwdriver, pliers,
birthday radio
bearing wire innards.
When anyone happens into you
at the bar, you never accept offers
of another Miller Genuine, never
linger later than nine at night.
There's always the shop to unlock,
desk phone loaded with voicemails,
a row of our cars—crippled

or bleeding flammably—
another morning whose sunrise copies
the lifting of brass from a cobalt box.

ODE TO KOOL-AID

You turn the kitchen
tap's metallic stream
into tropical drink,
extra sugar whirlpooling
to the pitcher-bottom
like gypsum sand.
Purplesaurus Rex, Roarin'
Rock-A-Dile Red, Ice Blue
Island Twist, Sharkleberry Fin;
on our tongues, each version
keeps a section, like tiles
on the elemental table.
In ninth grade, Sandra
employed a jug of Black Cherry
to dye her straightened
bangs burgundy.
When toddlers swallow you,
their top lips mustache in color
as if they've kissed paint.
The trendy folks can savor
all that imported mango nectar
and health-market juice.
We need factory-crafted packets,
unpronounceable ingredients,
a logo cute enough to hug,
a drink unnaturally sweet
so that, on the porch,
as summer sun recedes,
Granddad takes out his teeth
to make more mouth to admit you.

HOLDING CHANGE, AGE SIX

Mama gathered coins
from about our house
to count in the kitchen.
Across the quaky table,
her index slid
each minted disc
into glimmering mounds.
The fridge rattled—
in it, some milk
and a lettuce head
with a rust-spotted stem.
She allowed me to hold
a roll of 50 pennies
while we walked to the deli,
past a gas station, belled door
emitting a man who scratched
an instant ticket's
fluorescent parchment.

Molasses ham, peppercorn
turkey, burgundy salami logs
all propped cold
behind glass and priced.
Pointing to what we
needed, mama spoke
appropriate weights.
Our order parceled
in white paper, she nudged
me to lay the pennies
on the counter. Customers

shifted posture or sighed
in line, traffic lights
clicked commands, and I
squeezed the money
harder, copper bulk still
growing warm amid
the tiny trenches
and rifts within my fist.

VANTAGE

Just shaved, face
flawless like a waxed Cadillac,
dad peered into mirror, picking
his hair into a black globe.

Knee scar from playing 1-guard
for the Navy's hoop squad;
flat feet, stance
a smidgen bowlegged.

You might've been
one of our neighbors who wondered
how this man could actually love
my mama, a White woman
with Irish eyes, who
tilted into month-long moods.

You probably heard
their thunderous doors,
their fight-voices or
the snap of struck skin.

Maybe you squinted
through parted drapes to view
them tussle like two
tornadoes tied together.

Shame you couldn't see them
during certain days when
he'd stop her in the calm hall,

sweep a tress of hair from her neck,
and kiss her shoulder freckles as if
nothing ever made better sense.

HEARTBEAT BY WAY OF A BLUNT

Buy a half-dollar cigar; pull
    the red thread and disband
    its cellophane skin. Find
        the sharpest key on your ring, slice

lengthwise, like gashing the body of a bass.
    Nudge free the tepid tobacco
    so its outer leaf curls hollow,
        same shape as membrane

disowned by a snake.
    Unknot a 20-sack, bought
    at a house where dried peanut butter
        clings to mouse traps' triggers.

Fingernail stems and seeds away, tear
    buds to slivers that compose
    a pile of green commas.
        Once weed's sprinkled into cigar shell,

twist the rolled rug of it
    a definitive time, a woman
    correcting her skirt before departure.
        From the long lick you seal it with,

your tongue tingles.
    The childproof Bic clicks
    like cue against billiard ball.
        Smoke billows like a prairie signal;

wallpaper breaks
    an atom at a time from its glue;
    your heart is a fist
        something has tricked

to knock a century on the same door.

ODE TO THE BULLY

Your knuckles are rows of rocks
wrapped in dim skin.
Our collars crumple
in your indisputable grip.
Your footsteps unstem
elm leaves; your voice is
sledge-head against iron spike.
With our soda change and bus tolls
your pocket clamors
like the sea farer's purse.
You terrify our teachers,
your curse-laced refusals
rip their ears as if butcher paper.
Your mama some nights
doesn't come home
after tavern-waitress shifts;
she shuffles men
whose mouths know one motion
for winces and grins.
Your fridge is a bookshelf
after a literature burning;
your toilet and tub
are swampy, your room
drafty as a half-built boat.
Bully, we wish to be you,
to wake and flex our necks
loose of sleep's kinks,
to pull on cold clothes,
to trudge the street as sunlight
knifes the early sky,
to huff the neighborhood's nitrogen

and know about carrying out
the thorny vow, obeyed
from a basic age, to regulate
pain's imperative flames.

ADMISSION

Her small sisters asleep a room over,
a shy girl I knew from Civics class laid
a quilt on the floor because the bed would

give us away. Piece by piece our clothes dropped
into meek heaps, nightstand radio knobbed
to commercial-torn croon. A pull-chain lamp

snapped everything dark. The quilt bunched further
each time our bodies jolted together.
Streetlights, December trees, naked branches

glazed by earlier rain. I hiked alone
to an apartment where my friends perched—bowed
sofa, television with snowy feed.

Thirst-faced, they would need to hear how my first
night with a girl went. I sidestepped inky
puddles; a lie about feeling kingly

knocked to life in my mind, then a loud
wind kicked, thinning my coat to a sheet.
Rest of the way, I walked with my head down.

BREATH

My 73-year-old neighbor—
advanced emphysema, skinny
oxygen hose clamped

below his nostrils,
cylinder tank he dollies
throughout his hushed house.

I bring in his mail, pour
cereal or start coffee;
his lips fist at how much

less capable he is of the menial.
His wife of five decades
is four years buried.

He told me, shifting
the nightstand picture of her,
he misses her now no less than at first.

———

In childhood, during thick winter,
I wandered a field and found
a dead Labrador, mouth

frozen open so I could see
the two-colored tongue—
one more breath

the lone thing important
the moment intricate movements
inside him fell still.

———

First day of junior high
football, we ran
50-yard shuttle drills.

I crumpled
and grabbed the grass,
grandfather elms

throbbing in distance,
whole team's lungs
breathless as crushed boxes.

———

It's autumn, leaves
copper or maroon,
many breezes

flavored with cedar.
My neighbor
sits on his porch,

frail legs crossed
as he stares
past traffic until dark.

Teenage boys
gather at a corner
by a bus bench.

They puff menthols
pulled from a pleated pack,
talk about whatever

makes them feel braver.
Every one of their motions
is too new a music

to suspect their bodies won't
always conduct such
easy interplay with air.

RELOCATION

The Fredericks' youngest son
started running—ankle weights,
mornings peeling open
like books dried yellow from flood.

Coach lent him gym keys;
a 10-speed, kick-stood at the foul line,
portrayed a teammate's screen
(one he'd pivot around, shoot
15-footers as floor planks creaked).

Sophomore year he branched
to six-and-a-half feet, 210 pounds.
Daily, his mama's mailbox spilled
full-ride bids from as far as California.

Pegged fourth in the Pro draft, he penned
a contract, bottom-lined by
dream numbers.

Seldom, now, does his Range
Rover appear—thick-dish rims
like satellite alloy, truck body
low, a phonograph nose
needled to a road.

Not until the red halogen
of tail lights do we register
he grins mainly with relief—

not having to sleep again
on the acrid beds
the houses of our streets keep.

ODE TO THE PAGER

Your earliest versions
beeped like microwaves
or retreating trucks
or hospital monitors.
When cell phones cost
more than mortgages,
you clipped to our belt loops,
our pocket lips, our bookbag straps.
Fueled on Energizer alkaline,
your skinny screen delivered
numbers of souls
hankering for a word with us.
We'd bum someone's
touch-tone, or clatter
a quarter into a payphone, ear
suctioned to greasy receiver.
If our lovers intercepted
forbidden pages while we slept,
we woke to find you
drown in toilet water,
your display blotted opaque,
your heart a cracked cask of ink.
Without you, we missed parties,
managers curious
if we'd accept an extra shift,
younger sisters caught
in downpours across town,
parents who hadn't heard
our inflections in too long,
anyone who poked buttons and hoped

we'd be somewhere heeding you—
rectangular messenger
abuzz as a matchbox of wasps.

VALENTINE, 20-YEAR HINDSIGHT

Monica Malone, I'm sorry
for 1989, for the pharmacy-bought
valentine—Jordan dunking

on a cardboard heart, his jutting
tongue flamingo-wing pink.
I should've known a girl with curls

as well-oiled as yours
gets duffle sacks full
of love notes, candy baskets

from every brawny blooded boy
a factory town can spawn,
I should've known only

a pendant in a felt-skin shell
could've tempted your attention.
If, somehow, I'd attracted you correct,

we could've enjoyed a second grade date,
my mama could've scooped you
in our sandpaper Buick,

windshield crack shaped like a vein.
We could've chewed imitation
'Nilla Wafers, sipped purple Kool-Aid,

filament in the ceiling bulb tingling.
We might've seen our breath steam
while I toured you through

my neighborhood, maybe the alley
where a trashed cabinet lay
in gray snow, drawer-handle rust

the shade and grain of cinnamon.
Perhaps you would've tapped
your lips to my chilly cheek,

perhaps sky would've allowed
light through its bandages of clouds.
Perhaps it's perfect all of this

is contrary. You, now, with kids,
their ages near ours in 89', a husband
who speaks less each year,

and me, three lengthy states
plus a mountain range away,
still with this big divot on my center

finger, where the pen head rests, left
hand that's held and dropped multitudes
since the first wobbly words it wrote you.

FIRST SHOTS

Shaun's dad stashed a .25
in a bedroom drawer
with his wife's weekend jewelry.

One midnight they were away,
we stole the gun,
Shaun's eyes spacious

as we snuck to the park
and hopped the locked gate.
He triggered it first,

the back end of woods
where a possum wandered and clawed,
dragging its hairless tail.

When the hammer slammed
against the gunpowder capsule
at the bullet's butt,

my ear drums jumped,
then night wind slid into them
like velvet pulled through a ring.

After my turn we ran
the eight dark blocks home.
Beating his parents back,

we placed the pistol again
under folded socks, white shirts
looking never bothered.

When his folks finally walked in,
voices still notched to the volumes
of the bar they came from,

we faked sleep, our weapon hands
warm and awake
as if our fingers had combed a flame.

SPEECH THERAPY

Ain't nothin' wrong with double negatives.

All these teachers
pullin' proper grammar
around kids' ribs like a corset.

You breathe better
when your throat's welcome
to untunnel
the no's and not's that stockpile
during even a week a' heartbeat.

Speak with me.

We called everywhere
for Roberta Flack tickets
but nobody had none.

You don't got no brains, still
messin' with that reptile-eyed man.

Our building elevator only breaks
after you get groceries, never
when it's hardly nothin' in your hands.

You think you grown? Now on,
you bound to this house; don't even dream
about steppin' out, not nowhere.

I can't even talk to you no more.
No one knows
scarcely enough words
to keep track a' your triflin'.

WINTER THANKS

To the furnace—tall, steel rectangle
containing a flawless flame.
                    To heat

gliding through ducts, our babies
asleep like bundled opal.
                    Praise

every furry grain of every
warm hour, praise each
                    deflection of frost,

praise the fluent veins, praise
the repair person, trudging
                    in a Carhartt coat

to dig for leaky lines, praise
the equator, where snow
                    is a stranger,

praise the eminent sun
for letting us orbs buzz around it
                    like younger brothers,

praise the shooter's pistol
for silencing its fire by
                    reason of a chilly chamber,

praise our ancestors who shuddered
through winters, bunched
                    on stark bunks,

praise the owed money
becoming postponed by a lender
        who won't wait

munch longer in the icy wind,
praise the neon antifreeze
        in our Chevrolet radiator,

and praise the kettle whistle,
imitating an important train,
        delivering us

these steam-brimmed sips of tea.

DISCREPANCY

You don't own any suits
that cost less than my rent.
Your office perches at hawk's view;
mahogany paneled champagne fridge
to toast successful deals.

My mailroom radio trills,
speaker-mesh bleary
like a carpet layer's knees.

Your pupils trace ridged print
in *The Wall Street*; Japanese tea
calms your inner caverns.

I read Zora Neale,
gulp cafeteria coffee,
hors d'oeuvres of Cheeto or Frito-Lay
while Janie and Tea Cake work The Muck.

From your Tribeca residence, you can view
the Empire State Building
light nightly like a national candle.

At my D train stop, outside a turnstile,
a couple roars at each other
over a squandered Metrocard.

Could you contemplate a trade?

Your CEO salary
for the ingenuity of crunching
funds to settle the electric?

Your chauffeured Town Car
for an engine-rumped bus
with windows blanched by breath?

Monday-Wednesday-Friday chef
for scissoring coupons
and frying from a leased stove?

Eye-drying merger travel
for a broken-in couch
and bodega beer?

Calls walled with vacant talk
for a Marvin Gaye record
(evaporated ruby in your ear)?

Shuffle of annulment files,
the cufflinked filters that are your lawyers,
for a night with a woman whose skin
redeems anything the day means?

Notice how answers may not matter?

How earth simply picks
different specifics
by which it twists
each of us to dust?

NAVIGATION

Drive toward where night-clouds knuckle,
moon concealed
like a burglar's lucky pearl.

Miles unwind under your mismatched tires.

Engine valves swallow octane's protein;
radio static a dragging, long-straw broom.

What's out West?
Rushmore, Golden Gate, canyon,
river that keeps carving like a blind miner?

East?
Cities? Ports?
Snubbed lantern of winter?

The map refolds, roads jumble as if
a suitcase of sentences.

How many seasons
did you and that woman wish
to solve your love like an erratic crop?

How many more minutes
before your daughter wakes
in the back seat, milk-hungry, sun
rising just as answerless as always?

LATENIGHT INVENTORY

The jagged gravel
cradling these train tracks—
horizontal ladder attaching
our anthology of towns.

No more freighters for an hour,
no sooty cheeked conductor
navigating night, a thought
tied inside a sack.

The sky is tire-black, clouds
wiped away as if relic sand.

Lungs take licks
of tobacco smoke, pulse
purring like raked grass.

When the syllables of the word
America hadn't yet been welded,
someone surely stood here
as we do, escaped
from sleep's chalky grip,
breathing and figuring
how the moment fits
into the universe's
handlessly written list.

THE PASSING
—for Leo O'Connor

Grandpa's lungs and liver
cancerous, a nurse brought him
pills in paper thimbles.
His feet peeked from the sheets—purple
webs of veins risen to ankle skin.
He waved me close and spoke,
his voice soft as moss.

Mama picked a resting site
spread generous with birches.
In a pavement-gray suit,
dad cried while nearing the body—
grandpa had been the lone person
from mama's side to show
years ago when they married—
Black groom and White bride.

Outside an aunt's house after burial,
sun lulling into dusk,
with cousins I passed a football
(its main lace had unseamed, flapping
through the air every throw).

From the flimsy-railed porch, dad
stepped to where we played;
he capped my head with a large hand
and pulled me against his chest.
Breath bold with beer,
he said a slow sentence

about grandpa Leo and love,
then cast me back to the game,
to other boys with O'Connor blood,
streetlights watt by watt
rising as a choir of glare.

EIGHTH GRADE GRAMMAR

Mr. Bernard's bald scalp
glinted as if slanted glass.
With a bullet of chalk
his hand scurried the board,
writing what we were to recite:
"Jonathan went to the grocery store
to buy apples for Michael, his friend."
From an adjacent desk, Damon
leaned to me, whispering,
He always writin' on that board;
muhfuckah crazy.
Mr. Bernard heard, loosened
his neck tie and lettered
the next sentence.
Every morning he prodded
and spurred us through syntax
exercises, punctuation drills,
patrolling our haze-eyed ranks.
We bolted away as soon as June
delivered its pried crates
of lengthened days,
2Pac crackling from the black
foam of our earphones,
all our school papers
trashed like meaningless mail.
How would we have known
to merit a man who wore
inexpensive slacks, dense
spectacle lenses, a man given
nine months and city-bought books

that smelled of stale glue,
a man assigned to somehow
recouple the muddled
boxcars of our clauses,
to remeter our words
so the world might better hear us?

SUPPER

A coarse frost
claims the corners
of this morning's windows;

my uncle Clarence
wakes and showers
in an apartment he's lived in

alone seven years.
He drives a lumberyard forklift,
winter slashing into

open-ended storage caverns
he scuttles through;
now and then a glimpse

of sun, hazy gong face
fastened mid-sky.
After his shift's over,

the supermarket,
ingredients for dinner
jotted on scrap paper,

same pocket as his
dim-leathered wallet.
Home, he boils penne,

burner beside it simmering
a pot of tomato sauce;
chicken breasts broil,

grid that brands
black lines
onto meat's whitening skin.

He sits at the clothless
kitchen table, weighty
plate steaming

next to a glass
of apple juice with ice.
Life satisfies

in so many ways—
lying in a quiet room
alongside someone whose

touch you cherish, or a walk
at night through forest
wealthy with rustling leaves,

careful traffic of crickets,
earth recently rain-sweetened,
the never unremarkable

air of late May. My uncle takes
his first supper bite, eyelids
lowering like heavy petals.

Whatever stories we offer
about the vast facets through which
this world can quench,

we couldn't convince him
anything slakes
more than a worked-for meal.

WHEREABOUTS
—to Nicole

Finished early at the library,
    I strolled Canal Street to fill
    empty hours
before we'd meet home for dinner.

    Late-winter light sneered,
    reluctant to leave
the streets, bargain tables
    with t-shirts or imposter purses,
    jewelry coves
where gold necklaces refracted
    from squares of scarlet felt.

    All down Mulberry, arched
garlands of festival bulbs
    shined champagne.

    From Italian restaurant stoops,
waiters with handsome accents
    lured tourists by describing
    entrées like landscapes.

At Ferrara's dessert café,
    the wait bent
    halfway up the clogged block.
I whittled inside, browsed
    glass cabinets of cookies,
    yellow-shelled cannolis,
cakes displayed
on paper placemats
    that looked like lace.

I arrived 40 minutes late.
    You balanced, hand
    against bedroom door-jamb,
pulling off your office heels.

    Once you noticed the bakery box
    under my arm, your face calmed—
my earlier whereabouts
    evidenced in sweetness
    we would fork from the same plate.

HARLEM LANES

Columbia Students of Color
arranged a bowling party
on a Friday in February. A group of us
marched through slicing cold,
down 125th Street, sidewalk vendors
bundling merchandise for the night.

Inside, music thumped; women
we came with began dancing
before they tugged off coats.
We shared pitchers of beer—
the first sip left foam on someone's lip
like a shore just touched by tide.

We traded our shoes for red
and blue ones, entered names
into a keypad that fed a score screen
hanging above our lane. Past midnight
we shot at bottle-shaped pins,
we strutted or frowned

depending how many we knocked down.
I don't know if it's boring, or if it's a blessing,
how all us brown and beige and yellow people
did nothing more for hours
than laugh and dance and aim between gutters
during the brunt of winter in Harlem.

WHAT THE BADDEST KID IN OUR NEIGHBORHOOD SAID TO JASMINE JENKINS

I seen you catchin'
the morning bus for school;
I ain't gotta go cause I'm 16,
my mama ain't usually around,
and it's only been one
teacher my whole life
real enough to listen to.
Your mama and your pops
work at Chrysler, at least
20 a' hour, that's how they buy you
them designer jeans, that purse
other girls compliment
so they seem less jealous?
I bet a whole bunch a' dudes
try to talk to you delicate,
nervous voices askin' you to movies.
I like parties, music,
weed that would haze
space between us when we dance.
Everybody in this neighborhood scared,
careful cause they heard
I keep a gun on me like ID.
I don't need it; the idea's enough
for me to move through here easier.
Soon, I'll have enough paper
to buy that Monte Carlo
around the corner with tinted windows.
You could ride with me; I drive slow.

You gotta be smart with certain things.
Nice cars, pretty people
have you thinkin' that they stable,
but beauty so easy to break.

TONIGHT

Joanne: bowlegged like a wishbone;
  irises as tan as sand;
upper incisor cracked
  by a gone man's hand.

Her daughter crayons
  pages of a toddler book, lying
on a rug that has grasped
  the leaping seeds of fleas.

On the rear porch, Joanne,
  barefoot despite bitter wind,
lowers her head, sucks
  smoke from fragments of crack,

pipe glass burnt black, just enough
  breaths to patch the gap
between now and tomorrow.
  Soon she'll afghan her daughter

in the back bedroom, like a gardener
  patting loam closed again.
She'll sing fairytale lyrics, a mixed
  sack her memory sifts, voice

always half hoarse, daughter
  drifting open-mouthed.
I hope you'll be drinking later,
  in an overcast tavern,

when Joanne enters,
    ebony halter displaying
her angular frame,
    Vaseline-flattened hairline,

pinkie looped by a briny ring,
    exact ration of cash
for one clean gin.
    I hope you'll be there, for her

to turn and grin at,
    to target a stare at, her eyes
verifying there's nothing
    more important than tonight.

ODE TO LAST CALL

Shouted by the bartender
in a bill collector's baritone,
even the jukebox yields to you.

Our bottles and glasses grow
vacant as maxed-out mines.

Before you, we barked for hours
in varnished tongues, we bet
outcomes of pool table duels,
we laughed like rattling wagons,
we pissed in ceaseless shifts,
urinals centered with soap disks,
we chomped peanuts from plastic baskets,
steady snow turned the windows
to slowly unrolling scrolls.

Your lights flood our eyes,
push-broom us outside,
the night air a bitten plum.

Our cars wear cotton coats
we brush the windshields naked of.

Last Call, without you, how much
longer could we have eluded
our homes, people we trouble
and love, thoughts that luster
and rust, a world that swivels
tireless, as if its spin
won't ever encounter
the wall of the word Stop.

KISS

Saving money the summer
before moving to New York,
I painted houses during days,
nights in a restaurant kitchen
hosing dishes, loading them
into a steel washer that gusted
steam until two a.m.
Once, when I came home,
my back and neck bidding for bed,
asleep on the couch laid dad.
Flicker from muted TV
was the room's lone light,
but I could see his face fine,
broad nose, thick cheeks
holding glow as he breathed.
In five hours I would wake,
ride in the crew truck
to the assigned site,
gallon buckets and stepladders
chattering over road bumps,
axels clanging
like prongs of a struck fork.
Still, I stood and stared
at dad, a man
who poured four years
into the Navy during war,
who worked worse
jobs for shorter pay than me,
whose hands have blackened
fixing cars that quit

no matter how many replaced parts.
Above our house, clouds
polished moon as they passed.
Dad wriggled,
body pain or threatening dreams.
What else could I do
but bend down slow
and touch once
my lips to his brown brow?

ODE TO THE SCHOLARSHIP

You placate the stringent
landlord of the Registrar.
Your twinkling tweezers
pluck tuition's thousands

of thick splinters. You give
us a new room, suitemates
who doze too late,
whose towels hang dank.

You heap our trays
with cafeteria calories;
nozzled ice cream we spoon
until the bowl-bottom clanks.

We clawed like trapped hawks
to win you. We read our retinas
ragged, studied and notated
until the library's lights

died like gasless lanterns.
We triple-checked every speck
your applications incorporate,
we whispered prayers

and fed fat envelopes
to mail drops' mysterious mouths.
Of course the ducted salt of tears
upon the letter confirming you,

of course our mamas shrieked
to Jesus, of course local papers
ran features with our pictures.
Scholarship, think of the places

you diverted us from:
night corners at our birth blocks'
verges, police Caprices' locked
backseats, motel rooms

with dented lampshades, towns
where bone, muscle, and flesh best
most of the hidden electricity
our minds fight to emit.

MARY AT THE TATTOO SHOP

She counted her money
before we went in,
avenue beside us anxious
with Friday-evening traffic.
Both 14, we shared a Newport,
its manila butt salty to our lips.
Inside, from a huge book
of designs and letter styles,
she chose to get MARY
in a black, Old English script
on the back of her neck.
The guy who ran the shop
leaned over her for 40 minutes
with a needled gun
that buzzed loud
as if trying to get free.
He took her 25 dollars
then another 10
for being underage.
Back outside, the sun
dipped behind rooftops,
about to hand the sky over to night.
Lifting her hazel hair,
she asked me to rub
some A&D ointment
on her new tattoo;
my finger glistened in salve
as I reached for her swollen name.

POETS' CONDOLENCES TO CRITICS

Complete pity
your delicate skin forbids you

from the June sun strumming
every atom in this public park.

Sympathy for your keen
allergies, frenzied by the fine

green powder our children
kick airborne, running

and play-screaming through clover.
Our gravest laments extend

toward your diabetes, dismissing
this stocky slice of sweet potato pie,

auntie-baked, from an unwritten recipe
only family's allowed to learn.

RESIDENCE

Dislocated from sleep by alarm holler,
window light adamant as a sergeant.

Jobs and hustle reset the rent,
cupboards bank the grains,
freezer the meat if we're blessed.

Our addresses have shadows.

Our tongues take to song like salt.

From time-bowed photos,
elders squint against stricter
centuries' dust and sun.

In a basement,
a smuggled gun undresses.

A household's youngest
screams like ripping tin,
back teeth punching through his gums.

A woman inserts
earrings, dabs flammable
fragrance at her cocked neck.

The clock radio on the counter
dials to tunes introduced
by an igneous-voiced host.

While night steeps
the sky in deep ink,
just cinch your lips and listen
how us residents induce
selective heavens
to let our roofs lick
the original sugar of stars.

ACKNOWLEDGMENTS

My deep appreciation goes to the following press, publications, and websites where some of this collection's poems originally appeared:

Aureole Press, the chapbook *Rundown*, including "Admission," "Eighth Grade Grammar," "Freshman Audition," "Little Sister," "Tonight," and "What the Baddest Kid in Our Neighborhood Said to Jasmine Jenkins"

Blood Lotus (online): "Visiting My Great Auntie; Chester, GA"

Briar Cliff Review: "Holding Change, Age Six"

Cave Canem 2007 Anthology: "Harlem Lanes"

Cincinnati Review: "Speech Therapy"

Drunken Boat (online): "645 Phillips Ave." and "Poets' Condolences to Critics"

Evansville Review: "Supper"

Folio: "40 Ounce"

Georgetown Review: "What The Baddest Kid in Our Neighborhood Said to Jasmine Jenkins"

Hayden's Ferry Review: "Navigation"

Harvard Review Online: "Local Car Mechanic"

Just South Of Hell: "Kiss"

New Labor Forum: "Discrepancy," and "Ode to Kool-Aid"

The New Delta Review: "The Passing"

The New Yorker: "Mary at the Tattoo Shop"

Toledo Review: "15 Years Old in a Stolen Lincoln," and "First Shots"

CAVANKERRY'S MISSION

Through publishing and programming, CavanKerry Press connects communities of writers with communities of readers. We publish poetry that reaches from the page to include the reader, by the finest new and established contemporary writers. Our programming brings our books and our poets to people where they live, cultivating new audiences and nourishing established ones.